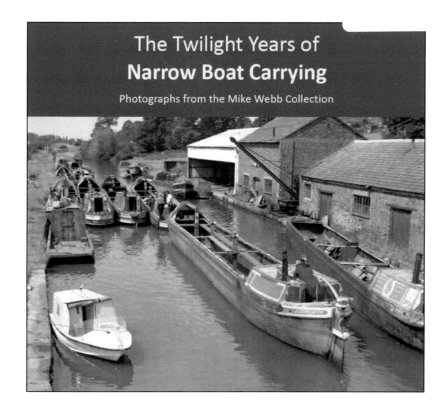

# The Twilight Years of
# Narrow Boat Carrying

Photographs from the Mike Webb Collection

**Foreword by Tim Coghlan**

**Introduction and photo captions by Pete Harrison**

CANAL BOOK SHOP

# The Twilight Years of
# **Narrow Boat Carrying**

## Mike Webb

### Photo captions by Pete Harrison

First edition October 2017
Canal Book Shop
Audlem Mill   The Wharf   Audlem   Cheshire   CW3 0DX

www.canalbookshop.co.uk

ISBN 978-0-9955180-4-9

# CONTENTS

**Front cover photo:**

Butty *Bedworth* with an unidentified motor boat leaving Braunston bottom lock and passing the dock of Willow Wren Canal Transport Services Ltd. on 16 July 1967.

# DEDICATION

My husband Mike's passion for canal photography began in the 1960s, all because he bought his first camera and because he was living near the S.U.C.

On behalf of Mike, I am certain that he would wish to dedicate these photos to people who are interested in the cargo-carrying fleet which he admired throughout his life.

I personally wish to acknowledge my gratitude to: Pete Harrison, for his continuous support when I embarked on Mike's Canal Archive, which is going to be passed to the National Waterways Museum at Ellesmere Port, and his meticulous checking for accuracy in this book; to Harry Arnold, for instigating the publishing; to Mike Pearson, for supporting me throughout the process; to Andy Worthington, Stephen Lee, Nigel Robinson, and to Clive Lloyd Jones for his encouragement, help and support from the very early stages. Finally, my thanks to Tim Coghlan of Braunston Marina for his sponsorship of this book, and to the publisher Peter Silvester at CanalBookShop, for his professionalism.

Thank you very much on behalf of Mike.

María Webb

**Mike Webb**
28 August 1934 - 14 September 2012

Biographical notes:
www.qr-memories.co.uk/mikegwebb

# FOREWORD
# Tim Coghlan

1963 was an ironic date in the history of English transport, with the two major rivals for so long, the canals and railways, both moving to the point of near collapse. In that year, the British Waterways Board largely closed down its canal carrying operation, and Dr Beeching announced his plans to do much the same to the railways. Whereas the railways were very accessible to the public, and were much recorded in those final years, the canals never really involved passenger carrying, and they remained to the end of carrying, a very private world of the working boatmen, which few outsiders, anxious to record something of their lives, were able to enter. One was Mike Webb, who not only patiently obtained the confidence and trust of the working boatmen, but was also a brilliant amateur photographer.

Mike Webb left the canals an outstanding legacy of well documented photographs, but he was a very modest man. Only a small number of his photographs have appeared in canal magazines and elsewhere over the years, and he was author to only two booklets, *Braunston's Boats* and *Shroppie Boats* published in 1983 and 1985 respectively, which both had small print runs, and have long been almost unobtainable.

I cannot recall ever meeting Mike Webb, though I am sure he would have visited our various Braunston Boat Shows and Historic Narrowboat Rallies, collectively dating back to 1991, with both events well attended by old working boats and surviving boatmen, whom he would have known. But we had a mutual friend in Harry Arnold MBE, a professional photographer and journalist, who also had been outstanding in recording the last working years of the canals.

Harry knew that I had been instrumental in persuading the late David Blagrove MBE to write his *Canal History of*

*Braunston*, which I had edited and helped source material and photographs for. That book, sponsored and published by Braunston Marina, was immensely successful. It went through two reprints, and then a new revised edition in 2004, and it is still readily available today – as I had intended. Harry tried on several occasions to persuade me to do the same for Mike Webb, or at least to have *Braunston's Boats* reprinted. But with so much else on my plate, it just did not happen. And then I heard sad news of Mike Webb's death in 2012, and thought that was that.

However, by good fortune, early in 2017, I got to know Peter Silvester of the CanalBookShop at Audlem Mill, who was beginning to reprint great canal books that were now long out of print, like Edward Paget-Tomlinson's classic *Colours of the Cut*. I discussed with him making a reprint of *Braunston's Boats,* which Braunston Marina would sponsor. I learnt that he was in touch with Mike Webb's widow María, who had many other photographs by him – most unpublished. Peter pointed out that a reprint would be impossible – other than from a scanned version of his original, but now 35 year old copy. This was because some of the original photographs were probably not available. His Plan B, with sponsorship from Braunston Marina, and working with María, was to compile a much thicker high-quality book, to incorporate a good collection of photographs from across the waterways, including some of the Braunston photographs that had appeared in that booklet. And where original photographs were in colour, to print them in that format, including several which were originally printed in black and white.

And here it is, over 150 pages of Mike Webb's wonderfully evocative photographs, with the captions by Pete Harrison, but based on Mike's own words, which together capture the twilight world of canal carrying in the 1960s. It brilliantly complements Sonia Rolt's *Canal People*, with her collection of Robert Longden's photographs of the central Midlands canals in the late 1940s and early '50s.

*The Twilight Years of Narrow Boat Carrying* is published with a good sized print run, that should keep it readily available for a few years yet. It is a wonderful tribute to Mike Webb to have his canal endeavours recorded in this way by María Webb and Peter Silvester, which Braunston Marina is proud to sponsor.


Tim Coghlan
Braunston Marina
October 2017

# INTRODUCTION
## Pete Harrison

The second half of the 20th Century was a time of change for the navigable inland waterways. Although the 1950s saw a slow decline in waterborne traffic, the business of canal carrying in the north west, midlands and south east continued much as it had for the previous 150 years. During this period the canals were still a private place, almost a secret world frequented only by those who had a direct connection, and those that had this connection often had family ties going back generations.

The decade that encompassed the 1960s changed these waterways forever, and these changes came from two separate directions. In the first half of the 1960s, trade continued to dwindle for a multitude of reasons, resulting in the inevitable termination of the large carrying concerns. This in turn led to the availability of redundant carrying boats at the same time as a general interest in canals spurred the canal enthusiast. Although canal enthusiasts had been around for several decades, they had been very much in the minority, with some working for the carrying companies and others having an interest in either pleasure boating or infrastructure.

The enthusiasts of this period provided a huge but unexpected benefit, as they often came equipped with notebooks and cameras, so capturing this period of change as the waterways, its infrastructure, its boats and its people moved from commercial to recreational use.

Mike Webb was one of these enthusiasts, who even as a boy took an interest in the Bolinder powered boats passing through his home village at Brewood on the Shropshire Union Canal. Over the following years, Mike made frequent visits to boating 'hotspots' around the Midlands, making notes and taking photographs at numerous locations between Preston Brook and Braunston. Mike's photographs capture a time that falls well within living memory, but the end of a different age, and encapsulate the 1950s up until the 1980s.

Mike was a highly respected enthusiast who operated in the background, and apart from two publications in the mid 1980s, his name was rarely spoken of. Mike was quite protective of his photographs, and although a few have been published, the majority in this book have not been widely seen before.

I hope this collection of photographs brings as much pleasure to today's enthusiasts as they did to Mike Webb.


Pete Harrison
Stockton on Tees
September 2017

**Opposite:**

The front cover of *Braunston's Boats*, published in 1983. © J. M. Pearson & Son (Publishers) Ltd., reproduced with permission. However, with a few exceptions, this chapter contains a different selection of photographs.

Mr & Mrs Sid McDonald aboard their butty *Bideford* on a glorious summer afternoon in 1967. Both *Bideford* and their motor *Badsey,* moored alongside, were still in British Waterways livery despite having been on hire to Willow Wren Canal Transport Services Ltd. for a number of years.

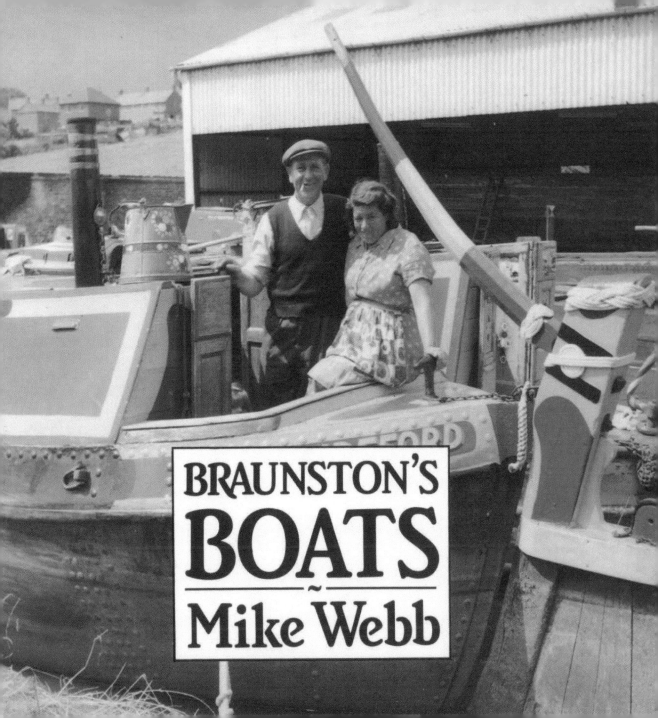

# BRAUNSTON'S
# BOATS
~
# Mike Webb

Butty *Bedworth* with an unidentified motor leaving Braunston bottom lock and passing the dock of Willow Wren Canal Transport Services Ltd. on 16 July 1967.

John Boswell aboard *Avocet* in 1963. *Avocet* had been built as *Raven* for Fellows, Morton and Clayton Ltd., and was purchased by Willow Wren Canal Carrying Company Ltd. in October 1954. At this time, *Avocet* was operating in the newly formed Willow Wren Canal Transport Services Ltd., and was powered by a 25hp Seffle.

*Jaguar* and *Crater* leaving 'Pub Lock' on 4 April 1965 with Ron Withey in command. This pair had loaded coal at Baddesley bound for the 'Jam Hole' at Southall. *Jaguar* was owned by Nicholas Hill (standing on gunwale), but was being operated by Seymour-Roseblade of Leicester. At the time of publication, *Jaguar* remains in carrying service with South Midlands Water Transport Ltd.

Tied up at Braunston with a full line of washing is the small Woolwich butty *Cygnus*, seen here with its 'captain' Ray White in the summer of 1964. Clearly the young lady is showing some enthusiasm towards her photographer. *Cygnus* was one of a number of boats leased to Willow Wren Canal Transport Services Ltd. by British Waterways Board in 1963.

The fore-ends of *Stratford* and *Bideford* about to come to rest against the gates of Braunston bottom lock in September 1961. These boats are in their blue and yellow 'British Waterways' colours, a livery that could be quite smart, although several boats from this fleet lost their yellow accents in the final days of 'British Waterways'. Both *Stratford* and *Bideford* were subsequently leased to Willow Wren Canal Transport Services Ltd. in 1963. The building to the left is a covered dry dock.

A bright day in February 1968, and just about to nose into Braunston bottom lock is the Blue Line Canal Carriers Ltd. pair *Stanton* and *Belmont*, with Jim Collins at the tiller. Blue Line were operating three pairs by this time, feeding coal from Baddesley to Kearley and Tonge, Southall then returning empty. As was common practice with Blue Line, this pair is breasted using the mast lines.

*Widgeon* and *Snipe* empty, and heading north into the second lock up at Braunston during September 1963. *Widgeon* was originally built as *Thaxted* for the Grand Union Canal Carrying Company Ltd., and *Snipe* is ex-Fellows, Morton and Clayton Ltd. *Kildare* (now back to *Kildare*, as butty to steamer *President*).

*Redshank* and *Greenshank* heading up Braunston locks. This pair was amongst the first to enter service with Willow Wren Canal Carrying Company Ltd., having being purchased from 'British Waterways' as *Reading* and *Bawtry* in February 1954.

Colette Wallace brings Birmingham and Midland Canal Carrying Company Ltd. pair *Yeoford* and *Pictor* out of lock 3 at Braunston, often known as 'Pub Lock', in August 1968. The vent in the engine roof shows that *Yeoford* was powered by an air cooled Petter PD2. Birmingham and Midland was a new company formed by enthusiasts, and at this time was, amongst other things, carrying coal to Croxley Paper Mills near Watford.

As *Widgeon* and *Snipe* leave lock 2 at Braunston in September 1963, they demonstrate the different dimensions of a large Northwich motor and a smaller F.M.C. butty (large and small refers to hull depth rather than length). Clearly these boats were not designed to work together, but the later days of canal carrying involved all sorts of mismatched pairings.

Ronnie Dell working the gate paddle of Braunston bottom lock in September 1963. Ronnie Dell had formerly worked as a boatman for 'British Waterways' prior to them terminating the majority of their carrying activities in the first half of 1963.

Doris Collins steers Blue Line's *Kent* and *Hazel* out of Braunston lock 3 in the early 1960s. Note that both boats are lettered as Blue Line Cruisers Ltd. Shortly after this photograph was taken, the Collins moved into the same Company's larger boats *Stanton* and *Belmont*. It was common practice amongst Blue Line steerers to run with the deck board in the hold when returning empty.

T. Humphries powers 'British Waterways' pair *Gardenia* and *Greta* through Cassiobury Park in October 1954. *Gardenia* was not completed until December 1947, and in this photograph is still carrying its Fellows, Morton and Clayton Ltd. livery, although the electrics were fitted by 'British Waterways' in October 1950.

Almost at the end of regular long distance carrying on the Grand Union Canal sees *Flamingo* and *Beverley* in July 1970. *Flamingo* was built as *Letchworth* for the Grand Union Canal Carrying Company Ltd., and was bought into the Willow Wren Canal Carrying Company fleet in December 1961. *Beverley* was on lease from British Waterways Board, and with a change of operator went on to carry commercially for a further 10 years as a rubbish hulk in the Black Country.

An unidentified 'British Waterways' large Northwich motor makes its way out of Braunston Tunnel in September 1961. The scrubbed cratch strings and belting can clearly be seen, a sign of a proud boatman.

A stoppage at Knowle locks in October 1961 has resulted in a queue of boats. An unidentified Thomas Clayton (Oldbury) Ltd. pair heads the queue, followed by a number of 'British Waterways' pairs including two 'blue top' butties.

Midsummer 1961 sees two early pleasure boats tied at the Samuel Barlow Coal Company Ltd. dock at Braunston. Both of these pleasure boats originated as commercial carrying boats, and were a sign of the change that was to come. This site is now occupied by Braunston Marina, and is almost the epicentre of the modern day pleasure boat industry.

Ray White takes a breather from unloading coke brought from Charity Dock, Bedworth, for use at Willow Wren's yard. The boat is *Dunlin,* whilst his motor *Crane* is tied behind, and the date is 4 November 1962. Emptying boats by hand was all in a day's work for a boatman, although there was often an extra payment for this back-breaking task.

Blue Line Cruisers Ltd.'s pair *Ian* and *Lucy* just starting to slow down as the boats enter lock 3, 'Pub Lock' at Braunston. *Lucy* had been built at Braunston in 1953 for Sir John Knill, a small independent carrier, and went on to carry with Blue Line until they ceased their carrying activities in 1970. *Ian* (later replaced by *Renfrew*) and *Lucy* were operated by the Whitlock family, with the motor often being steered by Laura Carter.

*Roger* and *Raymond* of Blue Line Canal Carriers Ltd. bring themselves into lock 3 at Braunston, adjacent to the Admiral Nelson public house, in March 1967. Arthur Bray is approaching the towpath side bottom gate and Ernie Kendall will be making his way up the steps to the offside bottom gate, although it looks as though they have plenty of onlookers for assistance, whilst Rose Bray watches from the hatches of *Raymond*. It can be seen how the mast line is being used to prevent *Raymond* from slipping backwards whilst tied abreast of *Roger*.

Heading away from lock 3 at Braunston in September 1966 is the empty single motor *Ascot*, captained by Geo. Lowe. *Ascot* was one of several boats on lease from British Waterways Board, and is seen here painted in a version of Willow Wren's livery. The dirty line along the hull gives some indication of how far down in the water these boats go when loaded. *Ascot* is still operating commercially as a fuel boat in the Milton Keynes area.

Ted Barratt Snr. heading south into lock 3 at Braunston on 8 May 1966 with *Sudbury* and *Barnes*. Although loaded with coal, it was sometimes a requirement to keep it dry, hence both boats are fully clothed on this occasion and on their way to Croxley.

Some narrow boats continued in commercial use long after their carrying days were over. Here we see ex-Willow Wren *Grebe* and ex-British Waterways *Water Ouzel* heading up Braunston locks in September 1966. *Grebe* had formally been a carrying boat in the Willow Wren Canal Carrying Company fleet, but transferred to their hire boat section, Willow Wren Hire Cruisers Ltd., when it became redundant in 1964. *Water Ouzel* was previously owned by 'British Waterways' and used as a Zoo Bus on the Regents Canal following its conversion from a carrying boat in 1959.

Mrs Violet Boswell with her children at Willow Wren Canal Transport Services Ltd. yard at Braunston in September 1963.

Wide beam motor boat *Progress* loaded with piles north of Boxmoor on the Grand Union Canal on 14 April 1956. *Progress* is wooden hulled and was built in 1934 by Bushell Brothers, Tring, in an attempt to introduce wide beam pairs on to the Grand Union Canal, but this proved to be unsuccessful, with narrow beam pairs operating until the end of carrying. *Progress* is currently the subject of a major restoration.

*Nutfield* and *Ara* pause as they pass up through 'Pub Lock' at Braunston on 21 November 1965. Both boats still carry their 'British Waterways' colours although they had been on lease to Willow Wren Canal Transport Services Ltd. for about eighteen months. Although these boats are starting to look down at heel, the cabin tops are very organised with everything in its place, and the stern fenders on *Nutfield* are high and proud just as they should be.

The cabin fire keeps the steerer warm on this frosty morning in February 1968 as Blue Line's *Stanton* and *Belmont* make their way towards 'Pub Lock', Braunston.

In contrast to the previous picture, this 1967 view of lock 3 at Braunston shows *Ian* and *Lucy* enjoying the sunshine, although it is obviously not that warm as Bill and Rose Whitlock, along with Laura Carter, are well coated. The spring line from *Lucy*'s mast to *Ian*'s fore-end is clearly visible, not to mention those sleek 'Nurser' fore-ends.

*Shirley* showing how 'British Waterways' altered their lettering prior to leasing to Willow Wren Canal Transport Services Ltd., by simply painting out the words 'British Waterways' and their lifebuoy roundel. Some boats remained in service painted like this for quite some time. On the end of the snubber, out of the shot, is the butty *Barnes*.

A family portrait taken on 14 August 1961. Mr & Mrs Mark Harrison, their children and dog, pose on their boats, motor *Quail* and butty *Kingfisher*. Both boats are built of wood. The butty, which had been built for Fellows Morton & Clayton as *Florence*, was at this time the only butty in the fleet with a forecabin. Soon afterwards, Mark swapped it for the bigger *Dunlin*.

Contrasting liveries in February 1968, with *Edgware* in its 'British Waterways' blue and yellow whilst butty *Capella* sports a variation of the Willow Wren livery. *Edgware* is powered by a Petter PD2 engine and the boats are running light as they head north out of Lock 3 at Braunston.

A fresh January morning in 1967 as the empty Birmingham and Midland Canal Carrying Company Ltd. pair *Yeoford* and its butty (possibly *Achilles*) enter Lock 3 at Braunston on their return from Croxley. This photograph helps to demonstrate that the boats did not stop as the weather deteriorated, and if they did stop, then there was no pay.

Willow Wren Canal Transport Services Ltd. *Coleshill* and *Cygnus* at Bancroft Basin, Stratford-upon-Avon in July 1964. The boats were captained by Ray White and they were attending the I.W.A. Festival of Boats and Arts in celebration of the re-opening of the southern section of the Stratford Upon Avon Canal. *Coleshill* and *Cygnus* came loaded with sugar and Honda motorcycles. An early pair of hotel boats is tied opposite.

Willow Wren's *Greenock* and *Bideford* entering Lock 3 at Braunston laden with coal in 1964.

Several boats laid up at Willow Wren's yard at Braunston. *Dipper* had been acquired in December 1961 from 'British Waterways', its original name being *Bristol*. The fuelling boom and its discharge pipe can be seen on the building opposite, and a pair lie in the 'fuelling berth' with the motor nearest the towpath.

Birmingham and Midland's *Linda* and *Barbara* head north, approaching lock 3, Braunston, in August 1965. *Linda* was completed in October 1931 as *Victoria* for Associated Canal Carriers Ltd., the fore-runner of the Grand Union Canal Carrying Company Ltd., and is commonly known as a 'Royalty Class'. *Barbara* is thought to be the short term alias of *Argon*.

Several Willow Wren Canal Carrying Company boats, including *Avocet*, *Sandpiper* and *Kingfisher*, laid up at their Braunston yard in August 1961. This Company acquired their boats from numerous sources, and boats originating from the fleets of Fellows, Morton and Clayton Ltd., Grand Union Canal Carrying Company Ltd. and Erewash Canal Carrying Company Ltd. are visible in this group.

Ernie Humphries brings his 'British Waterways' pair *Arcas* and *Actis* towards Braunston lock 3 in the summer of 1962. This pair was loaded with coal bound for Croxley Mill.

Almost home. Ernie Kendall steers *Nutfield* and *Raymond* towards lock 2 at Braunston in November 1968, very shortly after *Nutfield* had entered service with Blue Line. The lack of a 'tunnel hook' on the stern of *Raymond* necessitates the use of a spring line from the mast. Ernie Kendall and Rose Bray keep a close eye on the photographer.

Roger Hatchard on the well presented Willow Wren Canal Transport Services Ltd. motor *Hawkesbury*.

Birmingham and Midland Canal Carrying Company Ltd. *Linda* and *Barbara* flying down Braunston locks in August 1965. The use of one of the top cloths at the back end of the hold on *Barbara* allows for a slight cabin extension whilst the boats are empty, and the fore-end of *Linda* is so high when empty, it is fitted with a reduced cratch.

David Blagrove and Bill Fisher's *Enterprise* leaving Braunston bottom lock with the butty *Southam* in 1962. *Southam* had been acquired by Willow Wren Canal Carrying Company from 'British Waterways' who had used it as a rubbish boat in London. *Southam* did not enter Willow Wren's carrying fleet and was subsequently converted to a motor pleasure boat.

September 1963 - George Radford on *Baldock* and *Puppis* above Braunston bottom lock. These boats had been leased to Willow Wren Canal Transport Services Ltd. and George Radford had collected them. Both boats are wearing the last 'British Waterways' carrying fleet livery of plain blue, and the lettering is yet to be painted over.

Jim Collins prepares to bring Blue Line's *Stanton* and *Belmont* into Braunston bottom lock in February 1968. Bryan Nicoll's Watford based trip boat *Arcturus* is laying against the wharf and Willow Wren Canal Transport Services Ltd. *Cygnus* is against the towpath.

Below Braunston lock 3 in February 1968 are Birmingham and Midland Canal Carrying Company Ltd. motor *Collingwood* and Leicester Canal Transport's butty *Crater*. This pair was returning empty from Croxley Mill. *Collingwood* was not originally fitted with 'blue tops' as seen in this photograph, but had steel hoops every four feet or so over which a top cloth was drawn. It is said that the brackets that supported the steel hoops were removed as they obstructed the grab that was used to empty coal from the hold, and the 'blue tops' were a simple alternative.

Several boats tied at Willow Wren's Braunston boatyard, including the trip boat *Linda*. The corrugated shed housed a side slip and was constructed in 1962.

A frozen canal at Braunston in January 1966. The number of unoccupied, redundant and derelict boats is clear to see, and some of these craft were never to return to trade.

Blue Line Canal Carriers Ltd. *Roger* and *Raymond* head south for Southall in March 1967, co-steered by Arthur Bray and Nicholas Hill whilst Rose Bray looks on. It was common practice to tie the boats abreast when passing through locks that were close together, but some preferred to tow on a short line known as a snatcher.

Samuel Barlow Coal Company Ltd. sold *Gertude* in March 1961, and it can be seen here lettered in its new owner's name in September of the same year. Stephen Woolford operated *Gertrude* as a horse drawn trip boat at Thrupp near Oxford, although in years to come it was converted to a pleasure boat and motorised. Stephen Woolford must have had some success as in 1964 he bought the motor *Tyseley* and converted it to a restaurant boat, again based at Thrupp.

An undentified pair tied above Buckby top lock. The motor on the outside is a large Northwich and the butty is a small Woolwich. Clearly pleasure boating was becoming popular, as there is a centre cockpit cruiser tied behind this pair. Note the 'British Waterways' Austin A35 van.

The trip boat *Water Rambler* tied amongst Hatton locks in June 1961. *Water Rambler* had been converted out of the redundant motor *Star* by the Thames Launch Works for 'British Waterways' in 1957 and was used as a luxury trip boat for longer journeys, with passengers staying overnight in hotels along the way. When first converted, *Water Rambler* kept its original fore-end, but a section of this was later removed to aid better visibility for the passengers. The fore-end was rebuilt by its enthusiast owner in 1995.

Willow Wren Canal Transport Services Ltd. *Shirley* and *Barnes*. Both of these boats were on lease from 'British Waterways'.

Willow Wren Canal Transport Services Ltd. single motor *Halsall* captured passing through Braunston on 4 April 1965 on its way to Birmingham loaded with tomato purée. The captain is John Barratt. The 'T' stud on the stern of *Halsall* is a non-standard fitment.

Mark Harrison waiting to leave lock 3 at Braunston on Sunday 27 October 1963. The boats are Willow Wren Canal Transport Services Ltd. *Quail* and *Satellite*.

A resplendent *Nutfield* and *Raymond* captured in Braunston lock 3 in November 1968. *Nutfield* had only recently been commissioned into the small Blue Line Canal Carriers Ltd. fleet when this photograph was taken, and although usually a very private place, it is clear that Ernie Kendall kept the interior of *Nutfield*'s cabin simple in its decoration. A Torgem style coal fire replaces the cabin range.

The highly decorated cabin of Ted Barratt's *Hyades* on 24 January 1965. Although very traditional in its overall appearance, the cabin range has been replaced by a Calor Gas cooker and Torgem style coal fire.

Colette Wallace prepares the mast line in order to pull the bottom gate open of lock 3, Braunston, on a glorious summer's day in August 1968. The boats are Birmingham and Midland's *Yeoford* and *Pictor*.

Seymour-Roseblade's *Jaguar* and *Crater* edge into Braunston lock 3 under the control of Ron Withey on 4 April 1965. This pair was loaded with coal bound for Hayes.

*Curlew* and *Mallard* tied at Willow Wren's yard. *Curlew* had been purchased by Willow Wren Canal Carrying Company in 1961 and had previously been owned by 'British Waterways' as *Seaford*. *Mallard* was built as *Elm* for Erewash Canal Carrying Company Ltd., and was commissioned into the Willow Wren fleet in August 1954. *Mallard* was sold in 1966 along with the butty *Dabchick* for conversion to hotel boats.

'British Waterways' *Dubhe* and its motor (very possibly *Asterope* and under the control of Bert Wallington) heading north towards Norton Junction.

**Opposite:**

The front cover of *Shroppie Boats*, published in 1985. © J. M. Pearson & Son (Publishers) Ltd., reproduced with permission. However, with a few exceptions, this chapter contains a different selection of photographs.

**Top:**

Willow Wren Canal Transport Services Ltd. pair *Lindsay* and *Snipe*, captained by Ken Nixon, approach Wheaton Aston lock in 1967 with a diverted cargo of felspar for Dolbys at Stoke-on-Trent.

**Lower left:**

The legendary Charlie Atkins Snr. eases his motor *Mendip* into 'Cut End' (Autherley Junction) stop lock on a hot August day in 1961. Charlie had only just ceased carrying chocolate crumb from Cadbury's factory at Knighton to Bournville (a 14 hour trip each way) after 13 years employed exclusively on this contract; a feat which earned him the nickname 'Chocolate' Charlie.

**Lower right:**

The contrasting stern ends of Anderton Canal Carrying Co's motor *Shad* and butty *Aberystwyth* unloading silicone carbide destined for Stafford at Norbury Junction in 1968.

# SHROPPIE BOATS

## ~
## Mike Webb

Empty 'British Waterways' *Rudd* heads north past Brewood Wharf in August 1961 with Albert Hollinshead at the tiller.

Ben Smith's Thomas Clayton (Oldbury) Ltd. pair *Usk* and *Mole* head into Northgate top lock at Chester on their way to load fuel oil at Stanlow. Loading at Stanlow required these boats to venture onto the Manchester Ship Canal.

Norbury Junction was already a haven for pleasure boats in August 1966 when the Willow Wren Canal Transport Services Ltd. motor *Effingham* and butty *Keppel* passed through heading south loaded with 48 tons of bentonite for Wolverhampton. Jack Tolley shelters from the rain under a temporary canopy and *Keppel* is on the end of the snubber that can be seen disappearing back towards the photographer.

Anderton Canal Carrying Company's *Mendip* and *Shad* at Norbury Wharf in October 1968. Charlie Atkins Snr. looks on as he and the other boats await the unloading of silica sand.

As boats came out of full time carrying, most were adapted for use as pleasure boats of one sort or another. *Betelgeuse* was one of the last privately owned boats still carrying coal to Croxley Mill in 1970, but under the same ownership started operating as a 54 seat horse drawn trip boat out of Chester in May 1973. Here we see *Betelgeuse* on 9 August 1979 at Northgate, Chester, in a role it fulfilled until 1990.

*Parrot* and *Uranus,* loaded with aluminium, take a stop at Norbury Wharf in 1964. *Parrot* had been sold by 'British Waterways' to Peter Froud and Bev Portman in 1963, but had started its life as Fellows, Morton and Clayton Ltd.'s *Plover*. The re-naming took place in April 1952 shortly after its transfer from the south east to the north west. *Uranus* is still in its Samuel Barlow Coal Company Ltd. livery, but this boat was also acquired in 1963 by Peter Froud and Bev Portman.

Enthusiast owned *William* makes its way through the stop lock at 'Cut End' (Autherley Junction) on 26 August 1966. The boat patiently waiting behind is most likely the redundant Thomas Clayton (Oldbury) Ltd. motor *Spey* on its way to become a pleasure boat.

The towering fore-end of the empty Birmingham and Midland *Yeoford* passes Audlem Mill with its butty *Pictor* in June 1967. Note the loading gantry projecting from the Mill, removed soon after production ceased in 1970.

Midland Canal Transport's *Seaford* at the top of Tyrley locks in the early 1980s. Midland Canal Transport was made up of several enthusiasts who used their boats to keep trade on the waterways of the midlands.

Midland Canal Transport carried newsprint from Ellesmere Port to Brentford in the summer of 1985. Tony Gregory makes the difficult turn at Autherley Junction with *Tench* in May 1985, made all the harder by also passing a Simolda hire cruiser under the junction bridge.

'British Waterways' motor *Elk* cracking along at full chat. The position of the engine exhaust and the water trickling from the engine indicates this boat is still Bolinder powered. Note the unusual fleet numbering 735/35 along with the recent addition of a porthole in the cabinside.

Charlie Atkins Snr. keeps a close eye on *Mendip* as it passes through the gate narrows near Pendeford in September 1966.

*Tench* enters Tyrley top lock in 1982 with its owner Tony Gregory in command. Note the hand wound Klaxon horn mounted on the cabin slide.

In the developing days of Brewood Wharf, Mike Webb stands on the fore-end of Murray Jones' pleasure boat *Britannia* on 14 September 1961. The original identity of *Britannia* is uncertain, but it was eventually broken up at Tardebigge in the 1970s.

Birmingham and Midland Canal Carrying Company Ltd. *Linda* and *Barbara,* under the command of John Anderson, nearing lock 13 at Audlem. This was a trial load of 25 tons of aluminium from Walsall to Liverpool Docks and is dated 25 August 1965.

It became popular to convert redundant carrying boats to pleasure cruisers of one sort or another. Here we see *Agnes* in September 1961, a pleasure boat based upon a full length boat of north western proportions.

The single 'Admiral' motor *Grenville* passing through the village of High Onn in March 1967. These narrow boats were unique in having steel hoops across their holds which supported the top planks and top cloths.

September 1969 sees Anderton Canal Carrying Company's *Lamprey* approaching Wheaton Aston lock. The fore-end of the former Fellows, Morton and Clayton Ltd. motor *Daffodil* can be seen tied by the weir, having recently moved up from Aylesbury.

The heavily loaded Birmingham and Midland motor *Cypress* enters Audlem town lock (no. 12) in 1966. It was always advisable to use the side cloths when running this deep in the water.

*Tench* passes through Brewood in 1967 loaded with felspar. The boredom of single handed boating on long pounds is demonstrated by the wireless in front of the steerer.

*Linda*, owned by Birmingham and Midland Canal Carrying Company Ltd., passes a Double Pennant hire cruiser on its approach to Audlem lock 11 on 25 August 1965. The butty *Barbara* is following down behind, having loaded at Walsall a combined weight of 25 tons of aluminium ingots for Liverpool. The captain was Jack Anderson. The building by lock 10, which still stands, is known as 'The Shops' - workshops for blacksmith, stonework and woodwork for lock maintenance.

Birmingham and Midland Canal Carrying Company Ltd. *Linda* clears town lock (No. 12) at Audlem. Once the lock is empty, *Linda* will use a long line to pull in the butty *Ash*, saving on any bow hauling. This pair was heading for Oldbury in March 1967 with pitch that had been loaded at Liverpool.

With *Linda* having cleared Audlem town lock, it is now the turn of Birmingham and Midland's butty *Ash*, loaded with pitch from Liverpool, and bound for Oldbury in March 1967. Audlem Mill is visible in the background, with boaters' pub the Bridge Inn on the right.

Birmingham and Midland Canal Carrying Company Ltd. *Ash* about to leave lock 12 at Audlem in March 1967. The motor *Linda* can be seen in the distance ready to pull *Ash* out of the lock on a long line. *Ash* was originally built for the Erewash Canal Carrying Company Ltd., and the scrubbed belting and ropework on the helm can easily be seen.

Looking north across Norbury Junction in September 1961. An unidentified maintenance motor rests alongside the wharf.

Willow Wren Canal Transport Services Ltd. *Lindsay* with butty *Snipe* out of view, captained by Ken Nixon, motors south towards Wheaton Aston lock in March 1967. This was a diverted load of felspar bound for Dolbys at Stoke on Trent.

*Iona* was sold by Blue Line Cruisers Ltd. in the early 1960s, and by the time this photograph was taken it had been converted to a horse drawn day trip boat by Shropshire Union Cruisers at Norbury. *Iona* can be seen here heading north on one of its frequent pleasure trips, whilst the motor behind is very likely the ex-Fellows, Morton and Clayton Ltd. *Lily*.

*Yeoford* and *Pictor* from the Birmingham and Midland Canal Carrying Company Ltd. fleet tied at Norbury Wharf in September 1969. At this time both of these boats were fitted with tanks in their holds for transporting oil for Duckhams between Aldridge and Ellesmere Port. The first tanks to be fitted were not suitable and were replaced following a capsize.

*Effingham* and *Keppel* head south towards Norbury Junction in August 1966. Jack Tolley peers through his rain shellter as he steers the pair, loaded with 48 tons of bentonite, past the horse drawn trip boat *Iona* and other pleasure craft. The pleasure boat on the non-towpath side looks to be based on a wooden hulled B.C.N. day boat.

Washing day as the empty Birmingham and Midland's motor *Anson* heads down Audlem locks.

Canal Transport Services trip boat *David* awaits the lock to be emptied at Wheaton Aston. This boat was one of two wooden pairs built by Harland and Wolff in 1934-35 for the Grand Union Canal Carrying Company Ltd., and was originally *Aldebaran*.

The various twists and turns in *David*'s hull can be seen in this 1969 view as it awaits Wheaton Aston lock. Unfortunately this boat suffered damage in Bristol Floating Harbour in the mid 1980s, then dried out too much whilst awaiting repairs, so was subsequently broken up.

Charlie Atkins Snr. getting a crack on as he motors north near Brewood with the 'British Waterways' *Mendip* in the autumn of 1959. At this time, Charlie was working on the Knighton to Bournville chocolate crumb traffic for Cadbury Brothers, a job that earned him his nick-name 'Chocolate Charlie'.

Working down the Audlem flight from lock 3 to lock 4 with barrelled copper sludge from Darlaston to Manchester Docks. Mrs Radford steers butty *Beverley* beneath Bridge 76 whilst George takes the strain, having previously worked the motor *Tarporley* through lock 4. This is 1964 and the boats were leased by 'British Waterways' to Willow Wren Canal Transport Services Ltd., and although usually southern boats, they were on a temporary secondment to the north west.

Peter Froud and Bev Portman's pair *Parrot* and *Uranus* at Norbury Wharf in 1964. They were loaded with aluminium from Weston Point Docks and were heading south for Wolverhampton.

'British Waterways' *Anson* exits a bridge at Pendeford near the southern end of the Shropshire Union Canal in June 1961. At this time, *Anson* was paired with *Keppel* and under the control of the Tolleys.

Ex-Fellows, Morton and Clayton Ltd. motor *Clee* heading through Brewood and towards Wolverhampton on a summer's day in 1959. *Clee* was the last but one wooden motor to be built by F.M.C. Ltd. and passed into the 'British Waterways' fleet when only eighteen months old. Note the decorative ironwork on the fore-end, and even in 1959 there was a necessity to avoid canoes.

*Tench* loaded with felspar, and heading south through Brewood in 1967.

*Keppel* heads south and passes the Boulton and Paul factory to the north of Wolverhampton in February 1968. The 'signature' telegraph poles that follow the Shropshire Union Canal blend in with the factory chimneys.

'British Waterways' pair *Anson* and *Keppel*, laden with copper slabs for Wolverhampton, pass through canal maintenance works near Pendeford in June 1961. At least two of the maintenance boats are ex-Fellows, Morton and Clayton Ltd. motors.

An unidentified 'British Waterways' motor forges ahead through Brewood in July 1964. It was common practice in the north to roll the tippet down the deck board and secure it behind the headlamp as can be seen here.

A desolate Shropshire Union Canal in September 1969 as the Birmingham and Midland pair *Collingwood* and *Argon* pass a line of fishermen. The breeze across this open countryside creates a good drying opportunity for the washing rigged up on *Argon*.

Birmingham and Midland Canal Carrying Company Ltd. *Yeoford* and *Pictor* leave lock 13 at Audlem, making good progress towards the bottom of Audlem locks in June 1967. It is not unusual to lay the cabin chimney down when passing through locks, especially when light handed with low arched bridges.

The distinctive fore-end of Pimblott built Birmingham and Midland motor *Collingwood* with butty *Argon* heading south from Hack Green in September 1969. A feature of the 'Admiral Class' motors is that the base plate is upswept at the fore-end, leading to the stem being out of the water when empty.

The Trent & Mersey Boats section contains scenes ranging from the Cheshire Locks of the Trent & Mersey Canal to the south-western part of the Bridgewater Canal.

**Opposite:**

Most of the Anderton Canal Carrying Company fleet tied at Preston Brook in November 1968. *Shad* and *Aberystwyth* lay empty on the outside, awaiting orders. Most of the boats operated by Anderton Canal Carrying Company were on lease from British Waterways Board.

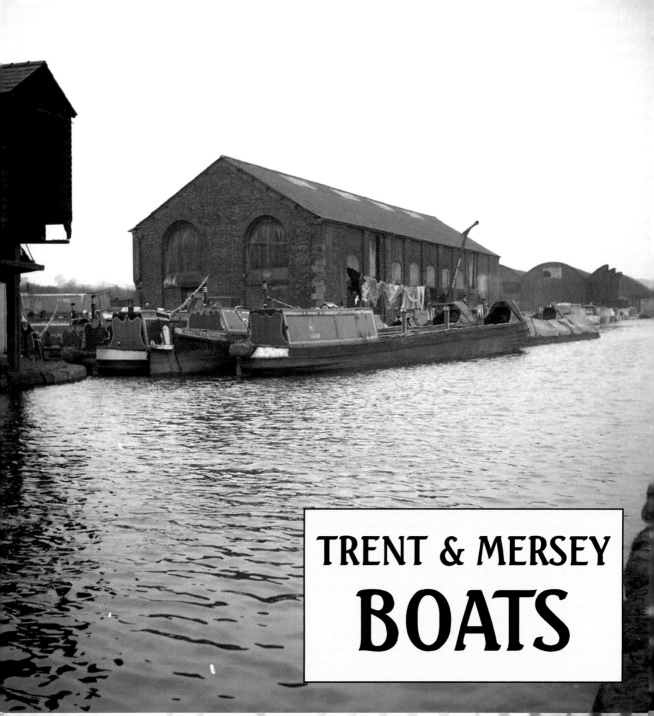

# TRENT & MERSEY
## BOATS

Ike Brace aboard 'British Waterways' *Tench* as it passes through Thurlwood Steel Lock in 1964. His butty *Birdswood* is in the brick chambered lock alongside (see right). *Tench* was originally powered by a 9hp Bolinder but was re-engined by 'British Waterways' with a twin cylinder 20hp air cooled Parsons Merganser, so making it more capable of working with a butty.

The 'British Waterways' butty *Birdswood* leaving the twinned Thurlwood locks on the Trent and Mersey Canal in 1964. *Birdswood* was paired with *Tench* which had just passed through Thurlwood Steel Lock alongside; they were operated by Ike Brace.

Anderton Canal Carrying Company's empty motor *Mendip* tied close to the top of Anderton Lift in November 1968. The footbridge to the left leads directly into Anderton Lift. Anderton Canal Carrying Company boats carried numerous liveries but this was their 'official' version.

Two redundant butties at the bottom of Anderton Lift in 1965. Nearest the photographer is 'British Waterways' *Ditton*, whilst the other boat is believed to be Willow Wren Canal Transport ServicesLtd. *Elton*. A few years later, *Ditton* went on to join Threefellows Carrying as a camping boat and *Elton* soon after passed to David Blagrove, with whom it returned to carrying service.

An impressive five boat line-up dwarfed by the larger boats of the River Weaver below Anderton Lift in the early 1960s. *Perch* is on the outside, with *Exeter* and *Pike* in the middle. The two inside boats are not identified.

Anderton Canal Carrying Company's *Lindsay* heads into the holding basin at the top of Anderton Lift in November 1968. The top cloths are drawn over the steel hoops down the length of the hold, giving a barrelled appearance. The top cloths were secured at the gunwale with a series of wooden wedges, and were unique amongst narrow boats to the 'Admiral Class'.

Heading south in 1964 is the 'British Waterways' motor *Malvern*, captained by Jack Tolley. The townscape of Middlewich can be seen in the background. This has changed considerably since the photo was taken, with little apart from the church and the canal now remaining.

Alan Galley of Anderton Canal Carrying Company leaving Anderton with *Lindsay* on route to Preston Brook in November 1968. *Lindsay* is still wearing the green and cream of its previous operator Willow Wren Canal Transport Services Ltd.

The fleet is in, November 1968. Most of the Anderton Canal Carrying Company boats at a wharf on the Trent and Mersey Canal. A number of sacks, possibly of bentonite, are visible in George Page's *Trout*, whilst the loaded *Keppel* lays alongside. *Mendip* sits high in the water, with another loaded motor on the outside.

Anderton Canal Carrying Company *Lindsay* waits in the holding basin above Anderton Lift in November 1968. The lack of cabin chimney and water cans suggest that *Lindsay* may be unoccupied, and on day work.

Laid-up motors *Malvern*, *Pike* and *Apple* in the holding basin above Anderton Lift on 13 June 1967. The boats were all leased by British Waterways Board to Willow Wren Canal Transport Services Ltd. Shortly after this photograph was taken, all three boats were returned to British Waterways Board, with *Malvern* becoming a canal maintenance boat, in which capacity it is still employed today.

Two 'British Waterways' boats passing up through Anderton Lift in September 1961. The contrast between the traditional running gear on the more conventional boat on the right with the modern hoops on the 'Admiral Class' motor on the left is clear to see.

The photographer looks down from the footbridge at the top of Anderton Lift as Birmingham and Midland Canal Carrying Company Ltd. *Linda* and *Barbara* approach on 26 August 1965. This pair was carrying a trial load of aluminium and was heading for Liverpool via Preston Brook.

'British Waterways' *Dory* at their Hayhurst Repair Yard in Northwich on 25 March 1957. *Dory* had been built as a Fellows, Morton & Clayton motor in 1934, but due to the 'British Waterways' policy of running pairs in the north west, a shortage of butties resulted in *Dory*, along with *Dace*, being converted to a butty. These conversions utilised the original underwater motor boat swim and built up the hull sides where the counters were removed. This was a simple but effective solution, but was not very attractive.

When awaiting orders, the Anderton Canal Carrying Company boats often tied at the top of Anderton Lift. Here on 13 June 1967 are *Shad* and *Aberystwyth* (Fred Gibbs) in the foreground, with *Effingham* and most likely *Keppel* (Jack Tolley) in the middle distance.

Two motors tied near to the top of Anderton Lift in the 1960s. Both are 'Admiral Class' and although loaded, appear to be unoccupied. Next to the towpath is *Lindsay,* with *Grenville* on the outside.

A posed photograph maybe, but this mother holds her daughter's harness reassuringly whilst on 'British Waterways' butty *Exeter* at the bottom of Anderton Lift in the early 1960s. The motor on the outside is *Perch*.

'British Waterways' boats at Lymm on the Bridgewater Canal in the early 1960s. These boats were operated by the Hollinshead family.

The Bridgewater Canal at Moore in 1963 sees several 'British Waterways' boats preparing to set off, including *Otter* and *Exeter*. It was common practice to tie boats together on long lines when working on the wide and deep Bridgewater Canal, and a line can be seen leading off the fore-end of *Otter* to an unseen motor. Note the early pleasure boat conversion to the right, very possibly Waterdale Canal Services *Hyperion*.

'British Waterways' Hayhurst Repair Yard on the River Weaver at Northwich maintained narrow boats of both their carrying and canal maintenance fleets. Here, on 23 March 1957, we see three former Fellows, Morton and Clayton Ltd. motors, including *Mendip* and *Clematis,* laying alongside the wharf in varying liveries . This was a busy time for Hayhurst Repair Yard as 'British Waterways' were in the process of modernising their fleet, including the replacement of Bolinder engines with more modern units such as the two cylinder Lister Freedom fitted around this time into *Mendip*.

**Opposite:**

Midland Canal Transport's *Tench* captained by Tony Gregory in the summer of 1983. Midland Canal Transport's *Tench*, *Lynx* and *Seaford* assisted by Doug Greaves *Otley* and Cliff Sherwood's *Bellatrix* transported 27,000 Ibstock bricks from the Daw End Branch of the B.C.N. to central Birmingham intended for the rebuilding of the towpath wall at Sheepcote Street Depot.

MIDLAND CANAL
TRANSPORT
No. 326

BRUMMAGEM
BOATS

'British Waterways' empty single motors *Mendip* and *Perch* frozen in above Wolverhampton locks on 2 February 1963. This freeze lasted for several weeks and bought the canals to a complete standstill. It was important to ensure you were in a good place when the canal froze, as those stuck in rural areas would struggle for water, coal for cooking and heating as well as for food.

Midland Canal Transport *Lynx*, *Tench* and *Seaford* assisted by Doug Greaves *Bordesley* loaded 70 tons of newsprint at Ellesmere Port on 24 May 1985 for onward delivery to Brentford. Here we see *Seaford* and *Bordesley* en route, steered by Doug and Jane Greaves. Newsprint is bulky, but not very dense, so the boats appear to be part loaded. The boats managed a return load of waste paper for reprocessing.

An industrial 1960s landscape at the bottom of Oldbury locks on the B.C.N. The factory to the right is Midland Tar Distillers, which was serviced by the boats of Thomas Clayton (Oldbury) Ltd., amongst others. An unidentified wooden motor lies outside redundant and sunken wrecks, and in the distance is a decked 'Claytons' family boat.

Cliff Sherwood's *Bellatrix* battles through the shallow backwaters of the B.C.N. whilst assisting Midland Canal Transport deliver Ibstock bricks to Birmingham on a late summer's day in 1983. The debris on the towpath gives some indication of what needed to be removed from the canal to get the boats through.

'Old' Joe Hollinshead slows his 'British Waterways' motor *Mountbatten* past Union Mill near Horseley Fields Junction on the outskirts of Wolverhampton in the early 1960s.

A posed 1960s photograph of Willow Wren Canal Carrying Company Ltd. *Trout* with George Page at the British Waterways Board depot at Broad Street, Wolverhampton. The circular plate near the pigeon box shows that the Bolinder engine had been removed, and replaced with an air cooled Lister HA2.

Stevens and Keay's rubbish hulks *Beverley* and *Bordesley* at Oldbury in the mid 1970s. These two boats were amongst the last to be carrying coal to Croxley Mill when on lease to Willow Wren Canal Transport Services Ltd., with the lease arrangement passing to Stevens and Keay in 1971.

'British Waterways' empty motor *Clematis* and loaded pair *Anson* and *Keppel* wait at the top of Wolverhampton locks in the early 1960s.

A view from Wolverhampton top lock with F.B. Lycett's pair *Bilster* and *Angel* on the outside of Willow Wren Canal Transport Services Ltd. *Effingham* on 20 April 1965. These were amongst several boats awaiting the unloading of aluminium.

Stuck again on the B.C.N. Several members of the Midland Canal Transport crew, friends and anybody else passing, work to free *Tench* as it runs aground during the delivery of bricks in the summer of 1983.

At least five B.C.N. day boats wait to be discharged of coal at Langley Forge. This was quite a common sight on the Birmingham canals throughout the 1960s.

George Clowes makes his way up Wolverhampton locks with the Thomas Clayton (Oldbury) Ltd. motor *Ribble*. Claytons sold *Ribble* in 1964; it was converted into a pleasure boat by a secondary school in Birmingham.

Looking towards Wolverhampton top lock and several 'British Waterways' boats waiting to unload in 1963. The nearest boat is most likely *Shad* with *Keppel* next to the towpath paired with *Anson,* and then *Clematis* on the outside.

Thomas Clayton (Oldbury) Ltd. *Ribble* with George Clowes in command continues his way up Wolverhampton locks in the early 1960s. In the latter stages of business, several of this Company's boats carried reduced lettering on their cabins as seen here.

Thomas Clayton (Oldbury) Ltd. motor *Tay* enters a lock whilst *Stour* hangs back. *Tay*'s engine exhaust size and position indicate that the original Bolinder 15hp has been replaced with something a little more modern. Claytons experimented with several engine types towards the end of their canal carrying operations.

Midland Canal Transport's *Lynx* pushed through the mud whilst loaded with bricks for Birmingham in 1983. *Lynx* was owned by Keith Christie and was powered by a Lister JP2.

There is almost no forward movement detectable as Keith Christie's *Lynx* makes its way along the Daw End Branch heading for Birmingham in 1983.

Thomas Clayton (Oldbury) Ltd. *Usk* with reduced lettering at the Company yard, Oldbury. This scene was obliterated by the building of a motorway a few years after this photograph was taken.

Birmingham and Midland Canal Carrying Company Ltd. boats await orders at Gas Street Basin in central Birmingham in August 1965. Gas Street Basin remained almost unchanged for another 20 years but is now unrecognisable, and yes, the plank was for getting across the narrows of the old stop lock.

Cliff Sherwood's always immaculate *Bellatrix* assisting Midland Canal Transport moving bricks across the B.C.N. in 1983. The bricks were destined for towpath repairs in central Birmingham.

Two 'British Waterways' pairs passing in Wolverhampton locks in early 1963. The uphill and loaded pair are *Otter* and *Aberystwyth* captained by Ralph Barnett, whilst the downhill empties are *Lindsay* and *Crewe* captained by Ken Nixon. Although *Aberystwyth* is still rising in the lock, the power is just on on *Otter* in order to keep the tow line taught and help open the top gate once the water level equalises.

The winter of 1962 into 1963 was severe, and here Ken Nixon's pair of 'British Waterways' boats *Lindsay* and *Crewe* are iced in at the top of Wolverhampton locks. This was certainly one of the harder aspects of boating, and drums up little in the way of romanticism.

Early in 1963, Ralph Barnett brings the 'British Waterways' motor boat *Otter* into Wolverhampton top lock, whilst at the same time altering the engine controls and manipulating the tow line back to his butty *Aberystwyth*. Although still in forward gear, the resistance of the water in the lock ahead of his boat will help bring it to a stop.

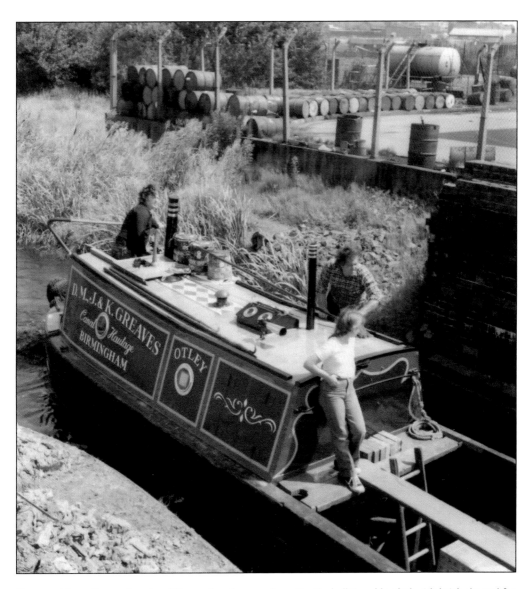

Doug and Jane Greaves' motor *Otley* makes its way along the Rushall Canal loaded with bricks bound for Birmingham in the summer of 1983. *Otley* was assisting Midland Canal Transport with this load, and the immaculate turnout of this boat was typical under the ownership of the Greaves family. *Otley* continued in trade for several years, and is the last boat to have been commercially loaded with loose coal tipped from a lorry at Tardebigge New Wharf, as late as 2002.

In memory of
**Mike Webb**
1934 -2012